VICTORIAN PICTURES

GUILDHALL ART GALLERY

ACKNOWLEDGEMENTS

This book by Vivien Knight, Curator of the Permanent Collection benefitted from the advice and assistance of staff in Guildhall Library. Stephen Freeth (Manuscripts) identified the Shakespeare quotation on page 6. The Victoria and Albert Museum provided information on the objects in Kate Hayllar's *Sunflowers and Hollyhocks*. Guildhall Art Gallery's conservators Cressida Harwood and Sally Woodcock supplied technical information on Watts's *Ariadne in Naxos*. Jeremy Johnson obtained all the photographic material and undertook the proof reading. First published in Great Britain in 1999 by Guildhall Art Gallery Publications

ISBN 1-902795-01-6

Cover: Dante Gabriel Rossetti *La Ghirlandata* (p. 37)
Title page: Kate Hayllar *Sunflowers and Hollyhocks* (p. 45)
Back cover: Sir Lawrence Alma Tadema *The Pyrrhic Dance* (p. 24)
Photographs courtesy of Bridgeman Art Library

Designed by Mick Keates
Produced by Supreme Publishing Services

THE TERM 'VICTORIAN PAINTING' describes many different kinds of picture, some with roots in the years before the Queen's accession in 1837 and others whose legacy extended beyond her death in 1901; the earliest picture illustrated in this book is dated 1832.

One of the most significant factors in the development of painting in the period was the growth of the urban middle classes. From these sprang collectors of art whose tastes – quite different from those of the aristocracy which had formerly comprised the art-buying class – spurred a vast production of historical, sentimental, humorous and narrative subjects. Under the patronage of the Prince Consort, the scheme to decorate the rebuilt Palace of Westminster with fresco paintings of subjects from British history and poetry fuelled public interest in contemporary art: the first exhibition of competition entries in Westminster Hall in 1843 drew thousands of visitors daily. The increasing demand for pictures by living artists was met by new picture dealers in modern art who began to develop in the 1840s their now familiar role of middleman between artist and patron.

One of the new middle class buyers who preferred living artists and familiar subjects to the dubious Old Masters that flooded the country was wealthy City port and sherry importer Charles Gassiot, who bequeathed his collection to Guildhall Art Gallery in 1902. Gassiot may have bought Alma Tadema's *The Pyrrhic Dance* in 1869 through the entrepreneurial dealer Ernest Gambart, but he acquired most of his pictures through Thomas Agnew and Sons, who opened in London in 1861 and came to dominate the art market. By publishing engravings after the most popular pictures Gambart and Agnew's made them inexpensively available to an even wider clientele. They also held regular exhibitions of British and continental artists, and as exhibitions of all kinds proliferated throughout London and the provinces, the Royal Academy found its monopoly challenged. Guiding the new patrons were influential exhibition reviews and art criticism in newspapers and periodicals (many new ones appeared in the period as literacy increased); the *Art Union* (later called the *Art Journal*) was the first specialist art publication to appear in 1839.

Interest in the Palace of Westminster scheme soon evaporated as the frescoes themselves decayed in London's corrosive air, but not before it had launched many artists' careers. Among the painters illustrated here who undertook paintings in the scheme were William Dyce (one of its organisers) and John Rogers Herbert. Both artists were influenced by the Nazarenes, a semi-monastic group of Catholic German painters working in Rome who favoured 'early Christian' subject matter painted with clearly defined contours in clear colours on a light ground. The Nazarene brotherhood had a British counterpart in the Pre-Raphaelites, who shared their interest in the Italian primitives and in mediaevalism. The Pre-Raphaelite Brotherhood was formed in 1848 in revolt against the art establishment and the Academy's conservative teaching. Although Pre-Raphaelitism was a coherent movement for only a few years, it was the most influential one of the period. The Guildhall Art Gallery collection includes William Holman Hunt's *Eve of St Agnes*, painted in 1847-8 just before the formation of the Brotherhood, as well as Dante Gabriel Rossetti's *La Ghirlandata* (1873), painted long after the break up of the group. (John Everett Millais' *The Woodman's Daughter*, of 1851, is illustrated in *Children in Pictures*.) Neither William Shakespeare Burton nor Henry Holiday were members of the Pre-Raphaelite Brotherhood but their pictures *The Wounded Cavalier* (1856) and *The Burgesses of Calais* (1859) demonstrate its pervasive influence in both manner and subject matter.

In the 1860s classical subjects became popular again, partly in reaction against the widespread influence of the Pre-Raphaelites. Edward John Poynter and Lawrence Alma Tadema – both trained on the Continent where Greek and Roman scenes by Gerome and his followers were already popular – were the first in England to paint accurately reconstructed views of ancient life. Poynter's *Israel in Egypt* (1867) incorporates meticulously researched buildings and sculptures, while Alma Tadema drew on copies from Greek vase paintings and his own library of photographs for the details in pictures such as *The Pyrrhic Dance* (1869).

A comparable urge for authenticity motivated the painters who travelled abroad in search of exotic subjects. In his *Early Morning in the Wilderness of Shur* (1860) Frederick Goodall paid as much attention to rendering the detail in a goatskin water bottle as Poynter paid in 1867 to the elements of his biblical construction or Alma Tadema to the details of armour worn by the hoplites in *The Pyrrhic Dance*.

The work of Albert Moore (1841-1893) offers neither an historically accurate version of the past nor any narrative subject matter, but fuses his interest in the Elgin Marbles with the subtle colouring of Japanese prints. Though small, *Pomegranates* was recognised by Moore's contemporaries as a seminal work in his development towards compositions that were simply vehicles for an exploration of formal elements and of colour. His intentions are far removed from classicing artists like Alma Tadema, and closer to those of the aesthetic movement, which had its roots in the discovery of Japanese arts and crafts in the early 1860s. After examples of Japanese design were shown in London at the 1862 International Exhibition an eager demand for Japanese culture and products developed in England, and masses of fans, parasols, screens, lacquer ware, ivory carvings, gowns and furnishings were imported for sale. This interest is reflected in G D Leslie's *Sun and Moonflowers* and Kate Hayllar's eclectic *Sunflowers and Hollyhocks* (both of 1889).

At the same time that Alma Tadema peopled his historical reconstructions with

'Victorians in Togas', James Tissot was displaying an interest in modern manners that parallels that of Trollope or Meredith. Tissot worked for *Vanity Fair* when he first arrived in London in 1871 and his modern life subjects like *Too Early* were inspired by magazine illustrations of society events. In 1865 the publisher Charles Knight complained that magazine illustrators depicted "every scene [...] where a crowd of great people and respectable people can be got together, but never, if possible, any exhibition of vulgar poverty. This view of Society is one-sided. We must look further for its 'many coloured life.' We want to behold something more than the showy make-up of the characteristics of the age. We want to see the human form beneath the drapery." However, it was generally held that realistic images of poverty were inappropriate in pictures intended to adorn living room walls; there was a thin dividing line between pathos and what was considered bad taste, and painful subjects had to be treated within certain conventions if they were to remain within acceptable boundaries. When Frank Holl's *The Lord Gave and the Lord Hath Taken Away* was exhibited at the Royal Academy in 1869 *The Times'* reviewer reassured his readers that 'the general effect, though intentionally sombre, is pictorially agreeable. The sympathies are powerfully appealed to, but the sentiment of resignation softens the pain and suggests its consolations'.

Guildhall Art Gallery acquired most of its Victorian paintings during the directorship of Sir Alfred Temple between 1885 and 1928. He was tireless in seeking appropriate works for the young Gallery, persuading private owners to part with their pictures and rich City individuals to pay for the paintings he bought himself on the Gallery's behalf. It was at Temple's urging that Charles Gassiot bequeathed the collection of paintings that still forms the core of the Gallery's Victorian holdings, while the pictures he bought from his own pocket included W S Burton's *The Wounded Cavalier* and William Holman Hunt's *The Eve of St Agnes*; only later was he reimbursed their cost by the men whose reward was to be acknowledged as their donors. Further examples have been acquired since Temple's death but it is largely to his efforts that the Gallery is indebted for its collection of Victorian pictures.

JOHN HENRY NIXON 1802-1857
Queen Victoria's Procession to Guildhall November 9 1837 1838

oil on canvas
Purchased from F H Nixon, the artist's son, 1880

William IV died in 1837 and was succeeded by his eighteen year old niece Victoria. On Lord Mayor's Day, November 9 1837, the new Queen dined at Guildhall with the new Lord Mayor, John Cowan, her procession from Buckingham Palace to Guildhall along streets filled with cheering crowds and houses decorated with bunting and greenery. In the City of London the Lord Mayor takes precedence over the monarch, and Nixon shows the procession passing the south side of St Pauls, led by the Lord Mayor holding the pearl sword point upwards and attended by the Common Cryer carrying the City Mace and the Swordbearer wearing the fur Cap of Maintenance.

The picture was exhibited at the Royal Academy in 1838 accompanied in the catalogue with lines from Shakespeare's *Richard II*:

> 'You would have thought the very windows spake
> So many greedy looks of young and old
> Through casements darted their desiring eyes
> Upon her visage.' –

> – 'Set forth in pomp,
> She came adorned hither like sweet May.'

It must have remained unsold because some years later Nixon sent it to the Mansion House, hoping that the Corporation would purchase it for £180. He died shortly afterwards, and it was not until his son tried to reclaim the picture in 1880 that the Corporation agreed to buy it for £80.

JAMES HOLMES 1777-1860

Charing Cross 1832

oil on canvas
Purchased from A Reader, 1950

A timid young woman is involved in a dispute with a hackney coachman over the fare; he holds out his hand for more money and motions the boy not to load her box, while a fashionably dressed young man intercedes on her behalf. Behind them a stage coach is about to leave for a country destination, the coachman raising his bugle to his lips to signify its imminent departure.

The scene is set in front of Le Sueur's statue of Charles I, with Northumberland House (demolished 1874) on the right. Most of the northern part of the Charing Cross area was levelled in the 1830s for the construction of Trafalgar Square, but roughly in the position now occupied by Nelson's Column stood the Golden Cross Inn which, though not included in this picture, stood to the left of the scene shown here. The Golden Cross was the major coaching inn of the west end, with both mail and stage coach services: Dickens had David Copperfield stopping there on his way through London to visit the Peggottys at Yarmouth, and perhaps Holmes's picture – with its strong narrative content – also illustrates an incident from an as yet unidentified novel.

ROBERT WILLIAM BUSS 1804-1874
The Crowd 1841

oil on canvas
Purchased, 1944

A cheering crowd looks down Pall Mall, with Wyatt's statue of George III behind them at the junction of Pall Mall East and Cockspur Street. On the banner fluttering from the house on the left the faint word *Victoria* above an indecipherable word beginning with *A* suggests that the occasion may be Queen Victoria's wedding to Prince Albert of Saxe-Coburg-Gotha in February 1840, when thousands of people packed the streets to see the royal procession from Buckingham Palace to St James's.

In 1836 Buss had produced three drawings for the second number of Dickens's serialised *Pickwick Papers*, and in *The Crowd* he displays the same interest in detail and incident that characterises Dickens's work, using the convention of the crowd to draw an amusing contrast between different classes and types of Londoner.

Ot the extreme left of the picture Buss introduces the hand of a pickpocket slyly lifting the dandy's watch and chain, while on the right the boys clinging to the lampost to get a better view are menaced by the fist and raised truncheon of an invisible policeman.

WILLIAM HOLMAN HUNT 1827-1910
The Eve of St Agnes: The Flight of Madeline and Porphyro during the Drunkenness attending the Revelry 1848

oil on canvas
Presented by Sir Charles Wakefield, Sir George Touche and Sir Francis Agar, 1924

The painting illustrates an episode from John Keats' poem *The Eve of St Agnes*, when Madeline and her lover Porphyro escape from her father's house during the festivities preceding the feast of St Agnes:

> They glide, like phantoms, into the wide hall;
> Like phantoms, to the iron porch they glide;
> Where lay the porter, in uneasy sprawl,
> With a huge empty flagon by his side.
> The wakeful blood hound rose, and shook his hide.
> But his sagacious eye an inmate owns;
> By one, and one, the bolts full easy slide:-
> The chains lie silent on the footworn stones:-
> The key turns, and the door upon its hinges groans.'

Hunt had discovered Keats in 1847, and felt this poem expressed 'the sacredness of honest responsible love and the weakness of proud intemperance'. (To emphasise the contrast he included the drunken revellers in the painting although in the poem itself they were asleep.) He began the picture on February 5 1848 for submission in April to the Royal Academy summer exhibition, painting at night by candlelight since he attended the Academy Schools by day. With its complex spatial organisation, striking foreshortening effect and contrasting light and shadow it was his first important painting – and the first he completed without using 'dead colouring', or underpainting.

In his memoirs (1905) Hunt recorded: 'The architecture I had to paint with but little help of solid models, but the bough of mistletoe was hung up so that I might get the approximate night effect from it: the bloodhounds I painted from a couple possessed by my friend Mr J B Price; my fellow student, Mr James Key, sat to me for the figure of the sleeping page and for the hands of Porphyro, so I was enabled to advance the picture with but little outlay.' Millais – in whose studio Hunt painted the picture – added the head of the bearded baron in the left background and the left hand of the reveller with thrown back head.

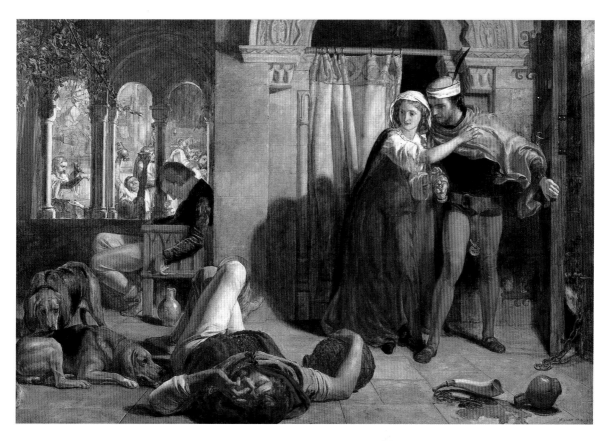

Sir Alfred Temple bought the picture from his own pocket in 1924, and was later reimbursed by Sir Charles Wakefield, Sir George Touche and Sir Francis Agar. Reporting its acquisition, Temple complained to the Library Committee that it had cost him 'a great deal of trouble and inconvenience,' but pointed out that 'it is by distinctive works of this character which mark the career and development of British painting, that a gallery like the Guildhall Gallery can not only be consolidated but made in the highest degree instructive.'

JOHN ROGERS HERBERT 1810-1890
The Youth of Our Lord 1856

oil on canvas
Presented by Charles Gassiot, 1895

There seem to be at least two other versions of the composition, so the Guildhall picture – which bears the date *London/1856* – may not be the version that was exhibited at the Royal Academy in 1847 with the catalogue caption

> 'Perhaps the cross which chance would oft design
> Upon the floor of Joseph's homely shed,
> Across thy brow serene and heart divine
> a passing cloud of Golgotha would spread!

and the note:

'The background is painted from a very careful drawing made at Nazareth.'

Herbert was a close friend of AW Pugin and at the height of the Oxford Movement he converted to Roman Catholicism, henceforth concentrating on Biblical subjects and adopting the clear outlines and colours of the Nazarenes.

The artist George Dunlop Leslie recalled Herbert painting the picture in 1847: '…my father took me up into the dome of the Academy [then in Trafalgar Square] to see him at work on his picture, which had been taken up there. Herbert was a confirmed smoker, and as he stated that he could not work well without a cigar in his mouth, the Council had allowed him to have his picture removed to the dome. I rather suspect that his real reasons for asking for this removal were to obtain the good light that the dome afforded, and the quiet privacy of the place. Herbert's hair was red, long, and very smootly brushed straight down; and he had quite a mediaeval look both in appearance and dress. The picture on which he was at work represented Our Lord as a boy, outside the carpenter's shed at Nazareth, carrying in his arms a basket containing long chips of wood, two of which have fallen on the ground in the form of a cross at which he turns and gazes. [...] It was exhibited two years before Sir John Millais painted his celebrated picture of 'The Carpenter's Shop', and I fancy that this picture of Herbert's must have had something to do with Millais' choice of subject. [...] He had not then adopted that strange affectation of always speaking with a French pronunciation which eventually became a confirmed habit with him…' (G D Leslie, *The Inner Life of the Royal Academy*, 1914)

The picture drew much critical praise, *The Times* noting that 'although characterised by German hardness, [it] breathes the most profound thought.' As Leslie noted, Millais took a similar theme two years later for his picture *Christ in the House of his Parents'* (1849-50), in which an accident at the carpentry bench foreshadows the wounds of the nails of the Cross.

HENRY HOLIDAY 1839-1927
The Burgesses of Calais 1859

oil on canvas
Presented by R W Allars, 1914

This was the young Holiday's first figure painting, begun towards the end of 1858 with a subject from Froissart's *Chronicles* – the sacrifice of six leading citizens of Calais who gave themselves as hostages to Edward III in 1347 in order to end the eleven month siege of the city. A townsman with a rope halter round his neck bids farewell to his wife in an interior

which Holiday painted from a room in St Paul's chapel at Westminster Abbey. The picture's Pre-Raphaelite appearance earned it mixed reviews when it appeared at the Royal Academy in 1859, *The Times* complaining of 'its determined antagonism to the ordinary conception of beauty,' but it established Holiday's reputation as a disciple of Pre-Raphaelitism.

RICHARD BURCHETT 1815-1875
Sanctuary 1867

oil on canvas
Bequeathed by E J Brett, 1895

After the last battle in the Wars of the Roses on May 4 1471 the beaten Lancastrians took refuge in Tewkesbury Abbey. Edward VI and the victorious Yorkists pursued them with drawn swords to the Abbey doors, where they were halted by a priest who abjured the King to spare the lives of those who had gained the sanctuary of the church.

Richard Burchett studied at the Government School of Design, and was successively Assistant Master and, from 1851, Headmaster of the Department of Practical Art. Absorbed both with his own teaching and in advising on the establishment of schools of art elsewhere he had little time to spend on his own history paintings, although with the aid of assistants he did undertake paintings in the Palace of Westminster scheme.

The picture was bequeathed to Guildhall by a children's magazine publisher with an interest in armour, Edwin John Brett (1828-1895), son of a British Army officer and the author of *A Pictorial and Descriptive Record of the Origin and Development of Arms and Armour* (1894).

WILLIAM DYCE 1806-1864
George Herbert at Bemerton 1860
oil on canvas
Bequeathed by Charles Gassiot, 1902

Although George Herbert (1593-1633) had a successful academic career at Cambridge and held the position of University orator for eight years, he retired from public life and was ordained in 1630. He obtained the small living at Bemerton, a village on the Avon one and a half miles from Salisbury in Wiltshire and there wrote the one hundred and sixty poems collected as *The Temple* which, he said, presented 'a picture of the many spiritual conflicts that have passed between God and my soul'.

William Dyce visited his friend Cyril Page, then the rector of the parish of Bemerton, in 1860 and painted this picture of the poet in his garden with its view across the water meadows to Salisbury Cathedral. Herbert was an accomplished musician, and his lute is seen leaning against the stone bench, the instrument perhaps also alluding to the lyricism of his verse.

According to Sir Alfred Temple (*Painting in the Queen's Reign*, 1897), Herbert is shown speaking the lines

> 'Sweet day, so cool, so calm, so bright,
> The bridal of the earth and sky,
> The dews shall weep thy fall tonight,
> For thou must die.'

The fishing tackle alludes to Izaak Walton, whose book *The Compleat Angler* (1653) included a quotation from this poem and whose biography of Herbert appeared in 1670. Temple claimed that Dyce originally wanted to show Herbert and Walton together, but on being told that they were not contemporaries removed the latter figure leaving in only his basket. As Herbert and Walton were in fact born in the same year and no painted-out figure was revealed when the picture was x-rayed, this story may be apocryphal.

WILLIAM SHAKESPEARE BURTON 1830-1916
The Wounded Cavalier 1855

oil on canvas
Presented by Lady Wantage, Lord Strathcona, Sir Edwin Durning-Lawrence, Bt,
Sir Charles Wakefield, Sir Julius Wernher, Bt, Sir Richard Stapley, Mr Walter Morrison,
Mr Henry Clarke and the Founders Company, 1911

The artist's father, William Evans Burton, gave up the family printing business in 1831 to go on the stage and in 1834 he abandoned his wife and child and went to America where he established a successful career as an actor-manager. His son could only attend the night classes of the Royal Academy Schools because he had to support himself and his mother by supplying drawings for printers and by working for Palsers, a firm of picture dealers in Covent Garden. He exhibited at the Royal Academy for the first time in 1846 and won the Academy's gold medal for historical painting in 1851 but it was *The Wounded Cavalier* that was his first and only great success in 1856.

A Puritan couple have come upon a dying Cavalier in the woods, and although he may have suffered his fatal wounds in an argument over a card game the young woman cannot help but comfort him while her disapproving companion stands stiff and helpless beside her: the viewer is invited to sympathise with the warmth of the girl's instinctive humanitarian response rather than with the man's chilly and rigid morals. Combining symbols of transience with a Pre-Raphaelite attention to detail the picture was begun late in the summer of 1855, in the grounds of an old cavalier mansion near Guildford (probably Loseley Park) where Burton placed his easel in a hole so he could study the ferns and brambles more closely.

When he submitted the picture to the Royal Academy exhibition it lost its label and was overlooked by the Hanging Committee (due, Burton claimed, to a conspiracy among the Academy porters whom he had refused to tip). It was found face to the wall by Charles West Cope who withdrew a picture of his own to make room for it, and was hung 'on the line' next to Holman Hunt's *Scapegoat*.

Without its label, the picture was unidentified in the first editions of the exhibition catalogue. Critics found the story unintelligible but thought the picture powerful and original. The *Art Journal* noted that it 'established his reputation: he is secure of fame hereafter', while Ruskin in his *Academy Notes* observed 'he seems capable of the greatest things.' Sadly these predictions were not realised. Burton's eyesight had been affected (he claimed) by his close attention to detail in this picture, and his next submission to the Royal Academy

was rejected: the disappointment, coupled with 'the continual strain of contact with his mother's difficult temperament', resulted in a breakdown. Throughout the rest of his life there were long gaps in his painting caused by harrowing events which included the sudden death of his first wife, a serious scalding, the death of his only child, and ever-present financial worries. He spent many years in Naples, returning to England only after his mother's death. In 1882 he suffered another breakdown caused by 'neuralgia of the brain.'

The Wounded Cavalier had been bought from the Royal Academy exhibition in 1856 by Agnews and sold to Mr J Arden of Rickmansworth. After his death Agnews bought it back and sold it to a Mr Albert Wood in North Wales. Temple persuaded Wood to sell him the picture for £750 and it was six months before he was reimbursed by the individuals named above as the donors. A subscription raised in 1911 enabled Burton to pass his last years in comfort but, as Temple recorded in his memoirs, 'one of the keenest pleasures he experienced was the knowledge that his one great picture was in the permanent gallery of the Corporation of London.'

MARCUS STONE 1840-1921
On the Road from Waterloo to Paris 1863
oil on canvas
Bequeathed by Charles Gassiot, 1902

One of a group of historical subjects in which he explored complex emotions or states of mind, this was Stone's first major success at the Royal Academy. Its subject was taken from a poem by Beranger, *Les Souvenirs du Peuple*, which he discovered while staying with Charles Dickens at Gad's Hill in 1862.

In 1912 Stone wrote in a letter to the Gallery: '*On the Road from Waterloo to Paris*, one of my early works, now in the Guildhall Gallery, was painted just half a century ago. I had lost sight of it for more than forty years, when I found it in the City collection. Looking at it almost as a stranger, I came to the conclusion that it was a somewhat remarkable achievement for a boy of 22, my age when it was produced.

'After the disastrous defeat of Waterloo, Napoleon with a small escort fled to Paris. Resting for a brief space he has entered a cottage & is musing by the fire. It was as you know wet weather. General Bertrand is drying the Emperor's coat (the immortal Redingote grise). A group of peasants stand aloof and gaze with awe and sympathy at their fallen idol. A young mother with a baby in her arms, a little girl and boy, a young widow and an old soldier with an empty sleeve. There is no man of fighting age, they have been drawn away for service in the campaign. A statuette of the emperor is on the chimney shelf, a print of him in his coronation robes is on the wall. Outside in the drizzling rain, the villagers are to be seen questioning the escort.'

SIR JOHN GILBERT 1817-1897
Fair St George 1880-81
oil on canvas
Presented by the artist, 1893

The mediaeval age was a major source for nineteenth century British art and literature, exemplifying the virtues of an 'Age of Faith' at a time when many perceived contemporary life as morally and spiritually empty. Here Gilbert depicts the well-known story of the 3rd century St George, who rescues the Princess Sabra from a dragon to which she has been abandoned after drawing lots and converts the citizens to Christianity before finally killing the beast which the princess has led back to her city with her girdle. This episode did not appear in the earliest accounts of the saint's life but it had become part of the legend by the 12th century and Jacobus de Voragine's *Legenda Aurea* (c.1260) established the story as one of Europe's greatest Christian legends. In 1484 William Caxton's English translation, *The Golden Legend*, was one of the earliest books to be printed in England.

Gilbert abridged some lines from *The Golden Legend* to accompany the painting in the catalogue of the Royal Academy exhibition in 1881: 'Smiting the dragon with his spear, he [i.e. the dragon] was sorely wounded and thrown down. Then St George called the Princess to bind her girdle about the dragon's neck and not be afeared. The dragon followed as it had been a meke beest and debonayre, and she led him into the city.'

Gilbert was a prolific illustrator for books, journals, newspapers and magazines (in particular *The Illustrated London News*), and an artist of oils and watercolours of historical and literary subjects. His warm colouring earned him the nickname 'the English Rubens', but while Rubens is recalled here in the appearance of the horse the figures of St George and the Princess suggest Renaissance sources such as Mantegna and Botticelli, as well as in Burne-Jones' 1865 series of paintings on the Greek legend of Perseus (the legend itself probably the original iconographic source for the story of St George and the dragon). The picture's format and composition – with its two close-up figures – is also reminiscent of Millais's *The Knight Errant* of 1870 and shares its somewhat erotic atmosphere.

Despite his earlier success Gilbert's pictures became unfashionable and in June 1880 he recorded in his diary: 'It is really no use painting; nothing sells. No one comes near me. There is such an utter stagnation that it is quite oppressive and disheartening. *Never* in my recollection have things been so *utterly bad*. In October he wrote: 'Painted again on St George in a fit of deep disgust and disappointment consequent upon the dreadfully depressed state of business. I turned it to the wall there to remain until the spring when

I propose to glaze it and finish it for the Royal Academy. No one has seen it. No one has been in my room since April last. *Horrible.*'

Fair St George remained unsold at £1,500 after the Royal Academy exhibition in 1881 even when Gilbert dropped the price to £900 two years later. In 1885 he decided to sell no more pictures but to leave them to the nation in a purpose-built gallery, a plan modified by 1893 when he invited the directors of several galleries to visit him and select works for their own institutions. He included Guildhall Art Gallery in the distribution after the President of the Royal Academy, Sir Frederic Leighton, told him that its recent exhibitions 'indicated a vitality in the City that can not be too warmly encouraged.' Alfred Temple, the Gallery's Director, was the first to arrive at Gilbert's Blackheath home, accompanied by the Lord Mayor and showing, as the *Magazine of Art* expressed it, 'their appreciation by a haste that under other circumstances might be called indecent'. Temple selected five oil paintings (including *Fair St George*), thirteen watercolours and thirty drawings – 'the cream of the collection' said the *Magazine of Art*, while the Lord Mayor of Liverpool who arrived shortly afterwards accompanied by representatives of the Walker Art Gallery had to admit that Temple had 'certainly secured the best examples'. A reception with music by the Band of the Coldstream Guards was held at Guildhall Art Gallery on May 17 to celebrate the display of the first batch of sixteen works, and the Corporation of London expressed its appreciation by presenting Gilbert with the Freedom of the City in a gold box. Temple and Gilbert became firm friends, with the result that a further fifty-three works entered the collection through the bequest of the artist's brother in 1903.

Sir Lawrence Alma Tadema 1836-1912
The Pyrrhic Dance 1869

oil on panel
Bequeathed by Charles Gassiot, 1902

This dance imitating the movements of attack and defence was performed in Athens and Sparta by armoured warriors: Alma Tadema suggests their movements with clouds of dust kicked up by their feet. They are watched by an all-male audience, those of high rank seated in front with those of lower status standing behind. The facade of a Doric temple with a polychromatic frieze can be seen behind the columns.

Alma Tadema visited Pompeii and Herculaneum on his honeymoon in Italy in 1863, and on his return to Antwerp abandoned his former mediaeval subjects in favour of the domestic genre subjects of classical – mainly Roman – life that were to bring him enormous fame. *The Pyrrhic Dance* – a rare Greek subject – was painted before the artist moved permanently to England but when he was already contracted to produce pictures for the dealer Ernest Gambart. Together with *A Lover of Art* (1868) it was the first of his works to be exhibited in England at the Royal Academy in 1869.

After *The Pyrrhic Dance* was included in Alma Tadema's retrospective exhibition at the Grosvenor Gallery in 1883, Ruskin made a vitriolic attack on it in his lecture on Classic Schools of Painting in *The Art of England* series of lectures at Oxford (1884). Remarking that Tadema's classical interiors were always represented in twilight, he continued: 'with that universal twilight there was also universal crouching or lolling posture – either in fear or laziness. And the most gloomy, the most crouching, the most dastardly of all these representations of classic life, was the little picture called *The Pyrrhic Dance*, of which the general effect was exactly like a microscopic view of a small detachment of black beetles in search of a dead rat'.

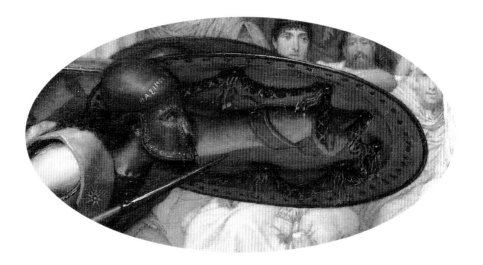

JOHN WILLIAM GODWARD 1861-1922
The Betrothed 1892

oil on canvas
Presented by H S E Vanderpant 1916,
from the collection of Lt Col Henry Louis Florence, (1843-1916)

Alma Tadema's meticulously recreated scenes of life in the antique world, particularly those depicting young women in marble interiors, earned him an enormous reputation and many followers. Godward was one of the best of these, bringing to his depiction of marble a skill approaching Alma Tadema himself. The composition of *The Betrothed* recalls Alma Tadema's own *In the Tepidarium* of 1881 (Lady Lever Art Gallery) but lacks its erotic atmosphere.

Godward was one of the many Victorian painters who survived well into the twentieth century to despair of the new kinds of painting and to see their own work derided. On December 13 1922 he was found on his studio floor with his head in a packing case and his mouth against the gas jets (pathetically, he had pinned a note on the door saying simply 'Gas').

ALBERT MOORE 1841-1893
Pomegranates 1866

oil on canvas
Bequeathed by Cecil French, 1954

The picture takes its title from the bowl of fruit in the centre. It combines the artist's interest in classical sculpture – especially the Elgin marbles – with the shallow space and subtle colours of the Japanese prints to which he was introduced by Whistler. Moore painted *Pomegranates* shortly after the outset of their friendship and the formal arrangement of its figures, together with its classicizing drapery and shallow, frieze-like space, reappears in Whistler's own *Three Figures: Pink and Grey* (1868, Tate Gallery).

Moore's careful painting method is clearly demonstrated in this picture. It was described by his friend and pupil Graham Robertson in *Time Was* (1931): 'When the studies had all been made, the first step towards the actual picture was the putting in of the whole composition in grey monochrome. Over this, when it was dry, came a thin, fluid painting very delicate in colour through which the grey design clearly showed. Next came heavy impasto, strong and rather hot in colour, over which, when dry, was passed a veil of semi-opaque grey, and on this was wrought the third and final painting, thin and delicate like the first'.

GEORGE FREDERICK WATTS 1817-1904
Ariadne in Naxos 1875

oil on canvas
Presented by Sir Marcus Samuel through the National Art Collections Fund, 1918

Ariadne was the daughter of King Minos of Crete. She fell in love with Theseus when he arrived among the sacrificial victims sent annually from Athens to be devoured by the Minotaur. With her help Theseus was able to kill the beast and escape from its labyrinth, and she begged him to take her back to Athens. When their ship was blown off course to the island of Naxos he abandoned the sleeping Ariadne on the seashore. Naxos was the favourite haunt of the god Dionysus, whose approach is signalled here by the leopards which drew his chariot and the gesture of the attendant. Dionysus determined to console Ariadne with the revelry and gaiety evident in Titian's version of the subject (National Gallery) but Watts chose to depict a still and drawn out moment in the story, Ariadne's sorrowing gaze and limp posture redolent of loss and betrayal.

This picture's very 'dry' appearance is the result of Watts' experiments with absorbent grounds and pigments ground stiffly with small quantities of oil medium, which he believed would render his pictures more permanent. (In fact the lack of medium means that his paint is poorly bound and often soluble.) Its colouring reflects that of Venetian painting, which Watts discovered when he travelled to Italy on winning a prize in the Palace of Westminster competition in 1843, while Ariadne's posture also recalls the pediment figures of the Elgin Marbles. Watts was attached to the story and produced other versions of this composition as well as single figures of the grieving Ariadne, but his wife, Mary Watts, in her *Annals* of his life (1917) reported that he described this work 'as the most complete picture he had ever painted'.

Temple had borrowed the painting from its owner Lord Davey for the first exhibition he organised at Guildhall Art Gallery in 1890. After Lord Davey's death it was acquired by Morland Agnew who gave it to the Red Cross fund raising sale held at Christies in April 1918, where it was bought by Sir Marcus Samuel (Lord Mayor in 1902 and later to become Lord Bearsted). Describing the picture as 'tender and beautiful', on the very last page of his memoirs Temple recorded his delight at its addition to the Guildhall collection. Perhaps it was at his urging that Sir Marcus Samuel bought the picture at the sale for presentation to the Gallery.

SIR EDWARD JOHN POYNTER 1836-1919
Israel in Egypt 1867

oil on canvas
Presented by Sir George Touche, 1921

Poynter took three years to paint *Israel in Egypt*, which illustrates a passage from Exodus (Chap 1 v 8) describing how the enslaved Israelites were used to build the store-cities of Phitom and Raamses. He depicts dozens of slaves dragging a red granite lion, lashed by an overseer shaded by his black servant. In the foreground a fallen slave is given water; at the rear of the procession an Egyptian princess shaded by a parasol holds up her small son.

Ahead, another lion is about to disappear through a distant half open doorway flanked by four colossal figures. A row of identical lions is visible in the unfinished courtyard beyond, with an empty base for one of those now being dragged in.

Poynter – the son of an architect – combines an eclectic collection of buildings and monuments from different sites and periods, depicting them individually with meticulous accuracy. Drawn both from published sources and actual monuments, they include the Great Pyramid from Giza, the temple and other buildings from Philae, the Obelisk from Heliopolis, and the Pylon Gateway from Edfu. The colossal back granite figures are based on those in the British Museum of Amenhotep III from Thebes. The Nubian lion is also in the British Museum, rows of similar lions had been exhibited in the Egyptian Court at the Crystal Palace in 1854.

Although some critics found its subject disagreeable and objected to the archaeological inaccuracy of combining elements found so far apart in reality, the picture was a spectacular success on its exhibition at the Royal Academy in 1867. It was bought by the engineer Sir John Hawkshaw who is said to have observed that there were not enough slaves to move the weight of the stone lion; it is true that Poynter added more priests and incidental figures and a few more pulling slaves after the end of the exhibition and before Hawkshaw took possession of it. After his death in 1891 the picture passed to his son John Clarke Hawkshaw, from whom Temple borrowed it for his Loan Exhibition of 1894. J C Hawkshaw died in February 1921 and it is tempting to surmise that it may have been Temple who suggested that Sir George Touche should purchase and present the picture in July. In October Temple told the Library Committee that Touche's 'magnanimous gift' was hung in Gallery 2, where it formed 'a very great attraction to the public'.

FREDERICK GOODALL 1822-1904
Early Morning in the Wilderness of Shur 1860

oil on canvas
Presented by Charles T Harris, Deputy, 1906

Goodall travelled to Egypt in autumn 1858 to look for source material for Scriptural subjects. On returning to England in summer 1859 he immediately began work on this ten foot canvas – his first Egyptian subject – which he titled *An Arabian Encampment at the Wells of Moses*.

The picture was an enormous success on its exhibition at the Royal Academy in 1860, and it was purchased by the wealthy shipowner Duncan Dunbar for 1,000 guineas. *The Art Journal* described the view: 'The site is towards the northern extremity of the Red Sea on its eastern shore. The view is therefore bounded by the Djebel Attaka, a lofty mountain chain on the west of the Red Sea, stretching northwards towards Suez. We approach the

work with a convction of its unimpeachable truth in every item of its principal and accessory features.' *The Times* too praised its depiction of 'the inner life of an Arab encampment, with its camel-hair tents, and tattooed women, and goatskin bottles and waterpots and yataghans, spears, matchlocks, and camel trappings, its hooded and kerchiefed Bedouins, bronzed Nubians, and recalcitrant camels, and in the midst a discoursing Sheikh, with an eager hawk-face, and an action like a John the Baptist preaching in the desert. Beyond the blue waters of the Red Sea rise the rose-flushed granite peaks of Djebel Attaka. It is a picture of magnificent colour and unadulterated desert life, with the stamp of recent and vivid impression upon every part of it.'

Although Goodall travelled again to Egypt in 1870, and enjoyed considerable success as an artist and establishment figure for the next 30 years, he never surpassed, or even equalled, this composition. On his death in 1904, describing him as 'a deserving artist who had outlived his popularity', *The Times* also observed that he had possessed 'much trained ability but no kind of inspiration'.

THE HON. JOHN COLLIER 1850-1934

Clytemnestra 1882

oil on canvas
Presented by Mrs Mary Harrison, 1893

Clytemnestra was the wife of Agamemnon, commander of the Greek forces which besieged Troy following the abduction of Helen. Before leaving, Agamemnon sacrificed their youngest daughter Iphigenia to ensure a favourable wind for his fleet. When Agamemnon returned, bringing with him Cassandra, the captured daughter of King Priam of Troy, Clytemnestra murdered them both in revenge. Clytemnestra and her lover Aegisthus were later murdered by her son Orestes, and the whole story is the subject of Aeschylus' trilogy the Oresteia.

Collier studied at the Slade under Poynter, and *Clytemnestra* reflects the desire for archaeological accuracy also found in Poynter's work. The composition includes a column from the Treasury of Atreus at Mycaenae (also known as the Tomb of Agamemnon), although Collier followed contemporary reconstructions of the doorway in erroneously placing the capital at its base.

The devouring and destructive female was an occasional theme in Victorian painting, and here Clytemnestra is shown with an expression at once triumphant and trance-like, pushing aside the curtain moments after dispatching Agamemnon with the bloody axe.

While this dramatic image generally reflects Collier's interest in the theatre, it may have direct origins in a performance of Aeschylus's *Agamemnon* given on June 3 1880 by Oxford undergradates at Balliol (with further performances at Eton, Harrow and Winchester schools). In this the part of Clytemnestra was played by a man – perhaps the source for Collier's unsettling, muscular figure.

EDWARD ARMITAGE 1817-1896
Herod's Birthday Feast 1868

oil on canvas
Presented by the artist, 1894

Armitage trained in Paris in the 1830s, a pupil of Paul Delaroche whose history paintings inspired him to concentrate on historical subjects, allegories and biblical scenes. *Herod's Birthday Feast* depicts the scene described in St Mark, Chapter VI, in which Salome, the daughter of Herod's sister-in-law and second wife Herodias, beguiles Herod with her dancing at his birthday celebrations. Armitage dwells on the exotic luxury of the feast and the allure of the dance rather than the earlier part of the story where John the Baptist tells Herod it is unlawful for him to take his brother's wife or the dramatic later part when Herod asks Salome what she wishes in return and at her mother's urging she asks for the Baptist's head.

DANTE GABRIEL ROSSETTI 1828-1882
La Ghirlandata 1873

oil on canvas
Purchased from David Croal Thomson, 1927

After Rossetti suffered a breakdown in June 1872 and took an overdose of laudanum, he was taken to Scotland to recuperate at houses belonging to his patron, Glasgow MP William Graham (1816-1885). In September he went to Kelmscott Manor in Oxfordshire, the house which he part owned with William Morris. Although Morris stayed away, his daughters and his wife Jane – with whom Rossetti was in love – were there, while among the visiting friends and models was Alexa Wilding who arrived towards the end of June 1873 to sit for *La Ghirlandata*. Rossetti described her to his mother as 'a really good-natured creature – fit company for anyone & quite ladylike, only not gifted or amusing. Thus she might bore you at meals & so on (for one cannot put her in a cupboard) but she is the most retiring of creatures and would not be much in the way, at least not more than was unavoidable'. At the top of the picture, the two angel heads were painted from Jane Morris's ten year old daughter May.

La Ghirlandata is one of several paintings of women playing musical instruments painted by Rossetti between 1871 and 1874 which loosely celebrate music or lyric poetry. He described it in a letter to William Bell Scott as 'the greenest picture in the world, I believe, the principal figure being draped in green & completely surrounded with glowing green foliage.' His intense use of colour creates a brooding pictorial mood, while the picture's symbolism – although unclear – may reflect Rossetti's unhappy mental condition at this time. In an article in the *Art Journal* in 1884 his brother William Michael Rossetti claimed that he had intended 'a fateful or deathly purport' through the dark blue flowers in the foreground, which were supposed to be the poisonous monkshood – although, 'being assuredly far the reverse of a botanist', Rossetti painted its harmless relative larkspur by mistake. The honeysuckle and roses around the top of the harp had a personal connotation of sexual attraction, while the harp itself represents music – a common metaphor for love and lovemaking. The climbing plant on the right resembles a clematis – its climbing, tendrilly habit perhaps symbolizing binding love.

La Ghirlandata was bought by William Graham, and when his collection was sold in 1886 Agnews bought the picture for 1,000 guineas and sold it to Lincoln engineer Joseph Ruston (1835-1897). At the sale of Ruston's collection in 1898 *La Ghirlandata* was bought back by Agnews, this time for 3,000 guineas, and sold by them to another engineer,

Scottish born James Ross (1848-1913) of Montreal. In 1925 Agnews suggested to Sir Alfred Temple that Guildhall Art Gallery might buy *La Ghirlandata*, but the suggested price of £4,000 must have prohibited further discussion. The picture reappeared at Christie's in July 1927, when it was bought by the dealer David Croal Thompson for only 800 guineas.

The enormous drop in value of Rossetti's picture in less than thirty years reflects the changes in taste in the new century which had by now seen not only French impressionism and post-impressionism but the Cubists, Fauves and Futurists among others; and after the horror of the First World War to many people painting like Rossetti's seemed irrelevant. However, in December 1927 the Library Committee accepted Temple's urgent recommendation and used its newly restored purchase of exhibits vote to buy the picture from Thompson for £1,200 (£600 down and the balance payable in the next financial year).

FRANK HOLL 1845-1888
The Lord Gave and the Lord Taketh Away –
Blessed be the Name of the Lord 1868

oil on canvas
Bequeathed by F C Pawle, 1915

Holl took the picture's title from the Book of Job, but its subject from Dinah Muloch's novel *The Head of the Family* (published in 1856). After the father's death, the eldest son – who has taken Holy Orders – pronounces a blessing over a frugal meal.

The artist's daughter A M Reynolds wrote in her *Life and Work of Frank Holl* (1912):

'My mother sat for one of the persons in the picture, a seated figure of a woman in black, her head drooping forward, the arm hanging listlessly by her side. My uncle also sat

for one of the figures. My mother has told me what an anxious time this was, my father being worried and nervous, and working feverishly at it every moment of the day. A difficulty arose as to the providing of a long-trained black dress which must be the garb of the woman in the picture, and it was only by dint of the utmost economy that my mother was able to get together enough spare cash to buy the dress, which she made herself. Great was the relief when the last touch was put to the picture. My father painted it *con furore*, and as the final stroke was added, put it face to the wall and, turning to my mother, said, 'Let's get out of here and have some air, I'm stifling!' As they went along towards Regents Park in the late October sunshine, they passed a coster barrow with some fine walnuts displayed – the first of the season. 'Let's have some walnuts,' said my father; 'the picture's finished, so let's give ourselves a treat!''

Although the setting is a bare room with a brick floor partly covered with a drab floor cloth, the artist takes care to show that the grieving family has not always been poor and tries to maintain genteel standards; *The Times*' reviewer approvingly noticed their 'long struggle of education and refinement with the most pinching poverty' when the picture was exhibited at the Royal Academy in 1869. Despite the women's undernourished appearance, the child's outgrown dress and worn out boots, and their meal of bread and tea (the diet of the poorest classes), their newly unfolded tablecloth is laid with a matching porcelain tea service and a bowl of flowers, the women's hair is neatly pinned and their old family servant is seen standing in the shadows at the left of the picture.

Holl submitted the picture for the prize of the Royal Academy's Travelling Studentship, which they were unanimous in awarding him in December 1869. By this time it had already been bought by Fred Pawle, a stockbroker from Reigate, Surrey and friend of Holl's father-in-law. Although Queen Victoria – herself in mourning for Prince Albert – had wanted to buy the picture Pawle refused to surrender it, and she was obliged to commission a different picture from the artist, *No Tidings from the Sea*.

James Jacques Joseph Tissot 1836-1902
The Last Evening 1873

oil on canvas
Bequeathed by Charles Gassiot, 1902

Tissot began painting riverside subjects soon after he arrived in London in 1871, drawn to the Thames by an interest in river and port life which stemmed from his childhood in the port of Nantes. As in other shipboard subjects, in *The Last Evening* he used seafaring friends as the models – John Freebody as the bearded captain and his wife Margaret and her brother Lumley Kennedy as the young couple. The setting may be one of the ships of which Captain Freebody was Master between 1870 and 1873 – the *Warwick Castle* and the *Arundel Castle*.

Tissot's father had run a draper's shop in Nantes and fabrics and costume play a significant role in his pictures; his use of pattern also reflects his interest in Japanese prints. *The Last Evening* is one of several paintings of c.1871-3 to show a black and white checked tunic trimmed with black ribbon; the red plaid shawl and the rocking chair were also favourite props.

The picture's story is ambiguous. The woman, perhaps an invalid, stares listlessly into

space as if oblivious of the ship's mate who gazes feelingly at her. Her father is presumably the old man speaking to the captain who watches the couple. Behind the men is a little girl who eavesdrops on both groups. None of the participants meet each other's eyes and Tissot uses sharp tonal contrasts and obsessively delineated rigging to create an oppressive and tense atmosphere.

James Jacques Joseph Tissot 1836-1902
Too Early 1873
oil on canvas
Bequeathed by Charles Gassiot, 1902

Tissot treats the theme of social awkwardness with affectionate humour. Coming to London in 1871 after the fall of the Paris Commune, he had stayed with *Vanity Fair*'s editor Thomas Gibson Bowles and worked as a staff artist on the magazine: *Too Early* was among the first of his immensely popular pictures inspired by magazine illustrations of society subjects.

The picture has an immediacy and informality that reflects Tissot's contacts with Degas and the Impressionists. All the participants – like the mistress instructing the musicians or the giggling maids peeping round the door – are caught off guard as if in a snapshot, a sensation emphasised by the way the spectacles of one of the musicians reflect the light as if caught in a photographic flash.

GEORGE DUNLOP LESLIE 1835-1921
Sun and Moon Flowers 1889

oil on canvas
Bequeathed by Charles Gassiot, 1902

The picture was painted from a window in the drawing room of Leslie's house at Wallingford on Thames where he lived from the 1880s, looking out over the garden to the meadow on the opposite bank of the river: he recorded that 'the whole was painted direct from nature'. One of the girls was a friend while the other was a favourite model of the artist's named Kitty Lambert. In contrast to the fashionable bustles and lacing of the period, they wear softer, more natural garments, in a reflection of the aesthetic taste which is also exemplified by the blue and white oriental vases, much admired and collected in the 1870s and 1880s, and in the sunflowers themselves.

KATE HAYLLAR fl. 1883-1900
Sunflowers and Hollyhocks 1889
watercolour
Presented by John Byram, 1963

Kate Hayllar, youngest daughter of the painter James Hayllar and the sister of artists Mary, Jessica and Edith Hayllar, painted this small picture at the family's home Castle Priory, Wallingford. The Louis XV chair and Elizabethan style table appear to be contemporary reproductions and were probably items in daily use at Castle Priory. The Chinese vases and Japanese screen indicate the influence at that time of oriental style on domestic taste.

Kate specialised in still life and flower subjects but she gave up painting around 1900 to become a nurse.

ANDREW CARRICK GOW 1848-1920
Queen Victoria's Diamond Jubilee Service, June 22 1897 1897-99

oil on canvas
Presented by Henry Clarke, 1899

The picture records the Service of Thanksgiving to com-memorate 60 years of Queen Victoria's reign which was held on the steps of St Paul's Cathedral on June 22 1897. Among the assembled dignitaries were the Archbishops of Canterbury and York plus fifteen Bishops and other rep-resentatives of the established church, many bishops from around the world, nine foreign ambassadors and foreign relatives of the Queen. The City's representatives included the Recorder, the Town Clerk and the Common Serjeant, while the small contingent of Aldermen and Common Council-men included Henry Clarke, one of those responsible for establishing the Guildhall Art Gallery twelve years before.

Clarke had offered to present the Gallery with a painting of the occasion and had chosen an artist identified by Sir Alfred Temple in his memoirs only as 'Mr B -' (perhaps J H F Bacon, 1868-1914). When Temple told him that 'B' would produce only an 'indifferent' picture and recommend-ed several other painters, Clarke commissioned Gow instead.

To enable Gow to sketch the scene Temple had a small enclosed platform built at the junction of Dean's Court and St Paul's Churchyard. The artist had to work swiftly because the service lasted only about twenty minutes before the royal procession moved on to the Mansion House. His movements were hampered by man employed to take photographs from the same viewpoint as well as the 'seething crowd of enthusiastic people' around him. As well as some small watercolour studies Gow managed to make a four-foot oil sketch on canvas which, said Temple, captured 'the local colour of the entire scene, but with of course no definite forms, only the very vaguest; there was no time.' These provided Gow with a colour record, but the static composition of the painting – which took two years to complete – seems to depend wholly on the photographs.

Index of Artists

Sir Lawrence Alma-Tadema (1836-1912) *24*

Edward Armitage (1817-1896) *36*

Richard Burchett (1815-1875) *15*

William Shakespeare Burton (1830-1916) *18*

Robert William Buss (1804-1874) *9*

The Hon. John Collier (1850-1934) *34*

William Dyce (1806-1864) *16*

Sir John Gilbert (1817-1897) *22*

John William Godward (1861-1922) *26*

Frederick Goodall (1822-1904) *32*

Andrew Carrick Gow (1848-1920) *46*

Kate Hayllar (fl. 1883-1900) *45*

John Rogers Herbert (1810-1890) *12*

Henry Holiday (1839-1927) *14*

Frank Holl (1845-1888) *40*

James Holmes (1777-1860) *8*

William Holman Hunt (1827-1910) *10*

George Dunlop Leslie (1835-1921) *44*

Albert Moore (1841-1893) *27*

John Henry Nixon (1802-1857) *6*

Sir Edward John Poynter (1836-1919) *30*

Dante Gabriel Rossetti (1828-1882) *37*

Marcus Stone (1840-1921) *20*

James Jacques Joseph Tissot (1836-1902) *42, 43*

George Frederick Watts (1817-1904) *28*

Index of Titles

Ariadne in Naxos (1875) *28*

The Betrothed (1892) 26

The Burgesses of Calais (1859) *14*

Charing Cross (1832) *8*

Clytemnestra (1882) *34*

The Crowd (1841) *9*

Early Morning in the Wilderness of Shur (1860) *32*

The Eve of St Agnes (1848) *10*

Fair St George (1880-1881) *22*

George Herbert at Bemerton (1860) *16*

La Ghirlandata (1837) *37*

Herod's Birthday Feast (1868) *36*

Israel in Egypt (1867) *30*

The Last Evening (1873) *42*

*The Lord Gave and the Lord Taketh Away –
Blessed be the Name of the Lord* (1868) *40*

On the Road from Waterloo to Paris (1863) *20*

Pomegranates (1866) *27*

The Pyrrhic Dance (1869) *24*

*Queen Victoria's Diamond Jubilee Service,
June 22 1897* (1897-1899) *46*

*Queen Victoria's Procession to Guildhall,
November 9 1837* (1838) *6*

Sanctuary (1867) *15*

Sun and Moon Flowers (1889) *44*

Sunflowers and Hollyhocks (1889) *45*

Too Early (1873) *43*

The Wounded Cavalier (1855) *18*

The Youth of Our Lord (1856) *12*